Frank Kessler

Prag und seine Umgebung

Frank Kessler

Prag und seine Umgebung

ISBN/EAN: 9783744647724

Hergestellt in Europa, USA, Kanada, Australien, Japan

Cover: Foto ©Andreas Hilbeck / pixelio.de

Weitere Bücher finden Sie auf **www.hansebooks.com**

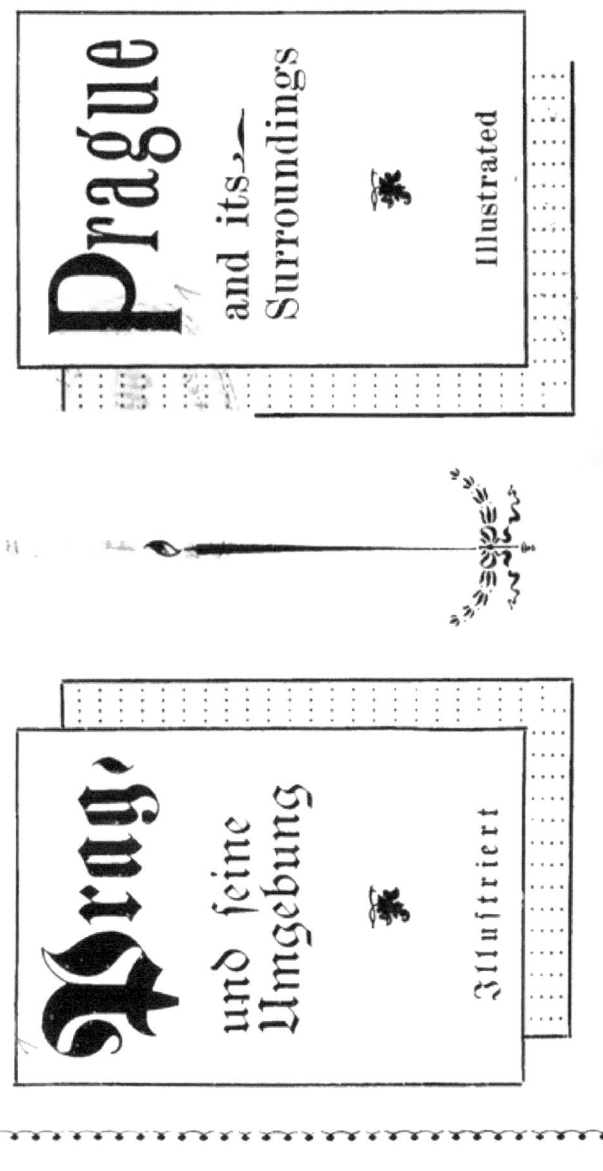

Prague
and its Surroundings

Illustrated

Prag
und feine Umgebung

Illuftriert

PUBLISHED BY
FRANK KESSLER
CHICAGO, ILL.
1898

KESSLER BROTHERS .. PRINTERS ..

Prague "
and its Surroundings

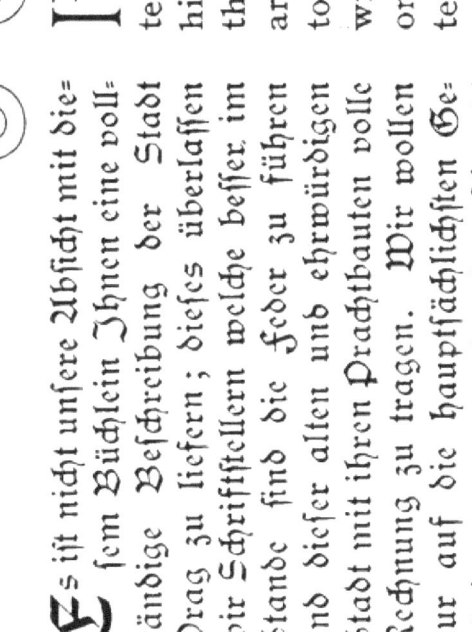

IN presenting you this little pamphlet it is not our intention to give a complete history of the city of Prague; this we leave to writers who are able to give due credit to this old and venerable city with its splendid edifices. We only wish to call your attention to the most principal buildings, of which you will

Prag ° ° °
und seine Umgebung

Es ist nicht unsere Absicht mit diesem Büchlein Ihnen eine vollständige Beschreibung der Stadt Prag zu liefern; dieses überlassen wir Schriftstellern welche besser im Stande sind die Feder zu führen und dieser alten und ehrwürdigen Stadt mit ihren Prachtbauten volle Rechnung zu tragen. Wir wollen nur auf die hauptsächlichsten Gebäude, wovon wir eine Anzahl

find a number of illustrations herein.

The Bohemian calls his native town the *golden* Prague, and justly so, — for this city captivates

The "Golden" Prague.

heart and mind of the visitor, that he soon feels at home and makes him part from the romantic valley of Moldavia with regret.

The most beautiful view of Prague is to be had from the terrace of the Hradschin, the Belvedere, or the look-out on the majestic Lawrence mountain.

First of all is the king's palace on the Hradschin, a group of

Ihnen bildlich vor Augen führen, aufmerksam machen.

Nicht mit Unrecht nennt der Böhme seine Vaterstadt das „goldene" Prag, denn die Stadt kann auch gar

Das „goldene" Prag.

gewaltig Herz und Sinne des Fremden bestricken, so daß er in Prag bald mit Leib und Seele zu Hause sein und das Scheiden aus dem wildromantischen Moldauthale ihm schwer werden wird.

Am schönsten zeigt sich Prag dem Auge, wenn man entweder von der Terrasse vor dem Hradschin, oder vom Belvedere, oder von dem Aussichtsthurm auf dem die Stadt majestätisch frönenden Laurenziberge Ausschau hält.

Panorama von Prag.   Panorama of Prague.

ancient buildings, the premonstrant abbey Strafow, the Rudolfinum, a splendid edifice, furtheron the magnificent churches and chapels, the churches of Thein, St. Peter, St. Nicholas, and St. Vitus, which are edifices that enchant the human heart. The cathedral is a splendid edifice of the french-gothic architecture, wherein the remains of St. John de Nepomuc rest in a three-fold silver casket.

The apostolic clock which was erected 1490 in the tower of the courthouse, was renovated 1864-65 at an expenditure of 4000 fl. This clock gives the time of the present as well as the old church calendar, the movements of the

Da ist zunächst das Königsschloß auf dem Hradschin, eine Gruppe alterthümlicher Gebäude, ferner die Prämonstratenserabtei Strafow, der herrliche Bau des Rudolfinums, dann die herrlichen Kirchen und Kapellen, die Theinkirche, Peterskirche, St. Niklas- und Veitskirche sind prachtvolle Bauten, welche das Herz entzücken. Der Dom selbst ist ein in französischer Gothik gehaltener Prachtbau, in welchem sich in dreifachem silbernen Sarge der Leichnam des hl. Johann von Nepomuk befindet.

An dem Rathausthurm befindet sich die 1490 verfertigte Aposteluhr, welche von 1864-65 mit einem Kostenaufwande von 4000 fl. renovirt wurde. Sie zeigt die Stunden.

Das Museum des Königs von Böhmen.　　Museum of the King of Bohemia.

planets and stars, the phases of the moon, commencement of the twilight, of the night and of the day, also contains a globe and a zodiac. When the clock strikes the windows above same are opened mechanically and the apostles Peter, Paul and John appear ; St. Peter raises his hand to heaven, St. Paul blesses with his head and St. John with with his hand.

Worthy of observation amongst the various bridges are the old Charles bridge, 500 metres in length and 10 metres in width, consisting of 16 imposing arches, resting upon mighty pillars, and ornamented with a tower at each end ; the Kaiser-

nach der heutigen wie nach der alten kirchlichen Zeiteintheilung, ferner die Planetenstunden und die Sternzeit, die Mondesphasen, den Beginn der Dämmerung, Nacht und des Tages und enthält die Erdkugel und den Thierkreis mit den Sonnen- und Mondzeichen. Beim Schlagen der Uhr öffnen sich die Fenster über derselben und die Apostel Petrus, Paulus und Johannes werden sichtbar; Petrus erhebt die Hand zum Himmel, Paulus segnet mit dem Kopfe und Johannes mit der Hand. Von den Brücken sind bemerkenswerth, die alte Karlsbrücke 500 Meter lang und zehn Meter breit bestehend aus sechszehn kühnen Bogen die von mächtigen Pfeilern getragen werden, und mit zwei

Franz bridge, constructed entirely of ..on, and the Palatzky bridge which connects the upper Neustadt with Smichow.

Prague has a great number of monuments, of which we call particular attention to the Radetzky, Jungman and Halek monuments, the Franzens monument on the Franzensquai, and the Charles monument on the Kreuzherrnplatz near the Altstaedter bridge tower.

The "Hradschin" or castlehill rises from the Kleinseite of Prague to a height of about 240 feet. The imperial palace, an irregular group of buildings crowns its summit, and

Thürmen an den Enden geziert ist; die Kaiser-Franzbrücke, ganz aus Eisen hergestellt, und die Palatzky-Brücke welche die obere Neustadt mit Smichow verbindet.

Auch an Monumenten ist Prag eine reiche Stadt. Es sind da das Radetzky-, Jungmanns- und Halek-Monumente, ferner das Franzens-Monument am Franzensquai, das herrliche Karls-Monument auf dem Kreuzherrnplatz unweit des Altstädter Brückenthurmes.

Der „Hradschin" oder Schloßhügel erhebt sich von der Kleinseite Prag's zu einer Höhe von etwa 240 Fuß. Der kaiserliche Palast, eine unregelmäßige Gruppe von Gebäuden krönt die Höhe, und

Der Graben.   The Graben.

is more remarkable for its location than for its architecture. It is claimed that the princess Libussa was the founder of same and that Charles IV. and others enlarged and beautified the palace.

In the court of the palace stands the cathedral of St. Vitus (which is a copy of the cathedral of Cologne), the erection of which was begun 1344, of which however but little outside of the gothic choir remains, but at present efforts are made to complete it. The tower which originally had a height of 500 feet, was destroyed to a great extend by fire.

Within the circuit of the pal-

---

ist mehr bemerkenswerth für seine Lage als für architektonische Bedeutung. Es wird gesagt, daß Prinzessin Libussa die Gründerin desselben war, und von Karl IV. und anderen vielfach vergrößert und verschönert wurde.

Im Hofraume des Palastes steht die Kathedrale St. Vitus, (eine Nachahmung des Kölner Dom's), deren Bau im Jahre 1344 begonnen, wovon aber wenig außer dem gothischen Chore geblieben, jedoch bestrebt man sich jetzt, dieselbe zu vollenden. Der Thurm welcher ursprünglich eine Höhe von 500 Fuß hatte, verlor etwa Zweifünftel davon durch ein Feuer.

Im Bezirke des Palastes befindet sich auch die St. Georgskirche, aus

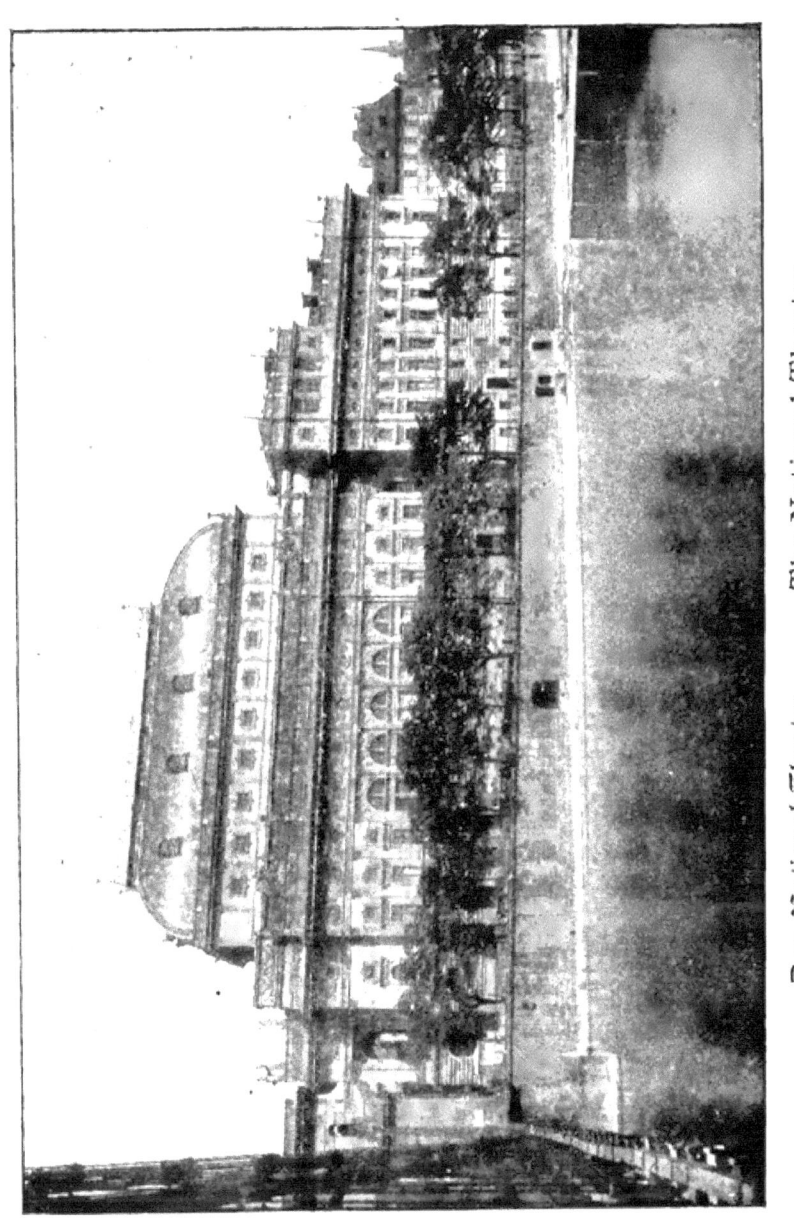

Das National=Theater.   The National Theater.

ace is also St. George's church, erected in the 12th century in the Roman style.

West of the imperial palace is a large square with three large palaces, of which one is that of the Archbishop of Prague.

Furtheron is another square, enclosed by the extended palace of Count Czernin (now a barracks), the great *Capuchin Monastery "Hradschin,"* and the church of St. Loretto.

With the Capuchin Manastery, wherein the monks have pursued art and knowledge for a great many years, is a large garden in which the herbs are cultivated that are being used in preparing

dem 12. Jahrhundert datirend, im romanischen Baustyl aufgeführt.

Westlich vom kaiserlichen Palaste befindet sich ein großes Gevierte mit drei großen Palästen, einer davon ist der des Erzbischofs von Prag.

Weiterhin liegt noch ein Gevierte, umgeben von dem ausgedehnten Palaste des Grafen Czernin (jetzt eine Caserne), das große *Kapuziner Kloster „Hradschin,"* und die Kirche St. Loretto.

Bei diesem Kapuziner-Kloster, woselbst die Mönche seit einer Reihe von Jahren der Kunst und Wissenschaft obliegen, befindet sich auch ein großer Garten, woselbst sie die Kräuter ziehen, welche in der

Der Hradſchin.   The Hradschin.

x

Der Veitsdom. Cathedral of St. Vitus.

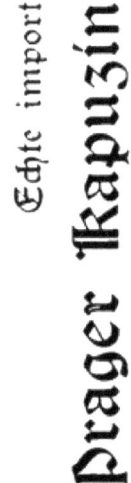

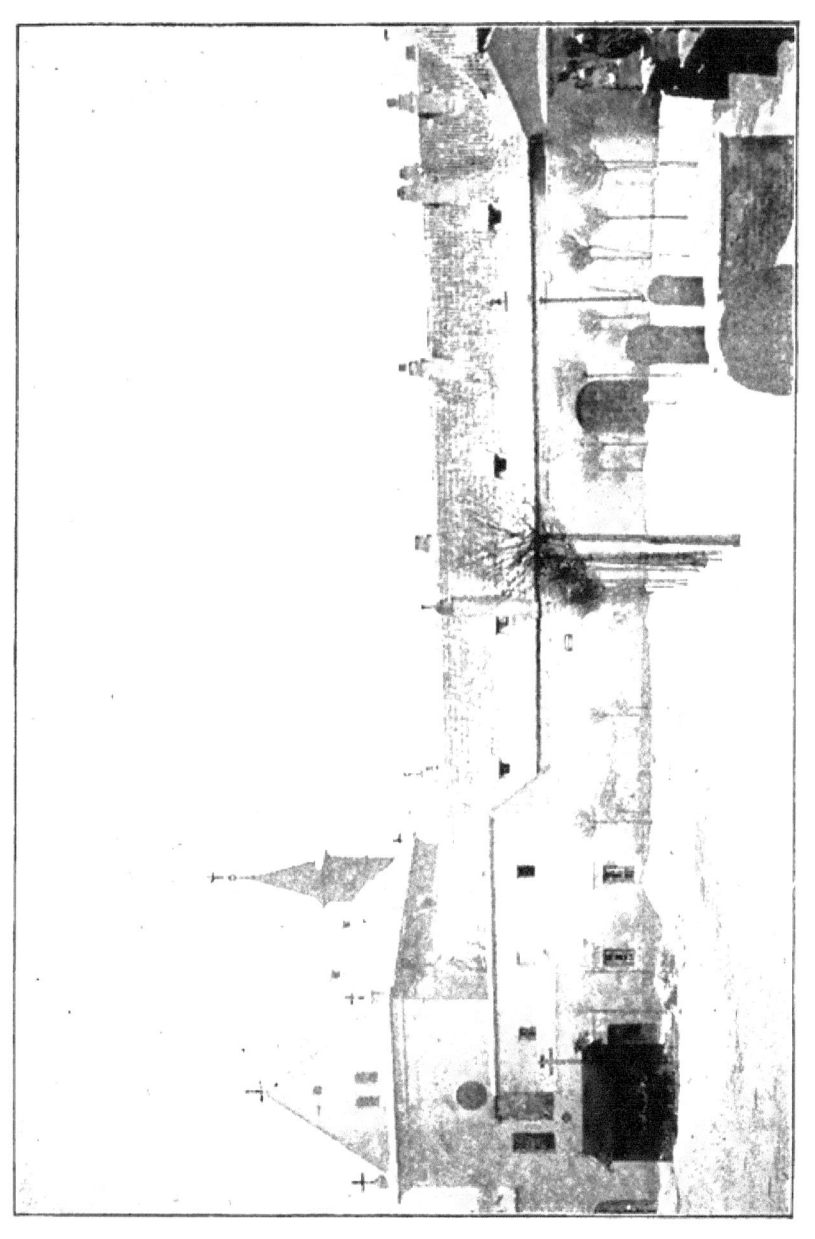

Das Kloſter Hradſchin.   The Monastery Hradschin.

FOR more than one hundred years the Capuchin Monks of the Monastery Hradschin, near Prague, have prepared a remedy, which on account of its superior qualities, seeks its equal.

It is a remedy, which, through this long term of years, became known as the celebrated CAPUCHIN DROPS, a medicine prepared from the herbs which are cultivated in the large gardens adjoining the monastery.

Experience has taught us that medicines, prepared from vegetable substances, are by far more beneficial to the human system, than such which contain mineral substances.

Seit mehr als hundert Jahren wird von den Kapuziner-Mönchen im Kloster Hradschin bei Prag, eine Arznei hergestellt, welche ihrer vortrefflichen Eigenschaften wegen ihres gleichen sucht. Es sind die während dieser langen Reihe von Jahren so berühmt gewordenen Kapuziner-Tropfen, eine Medizin welche aus Kräutern besteht die in dem großen, sich dem Kloster angrenzenden Garten, gezogen werden.

Die Erfahrung hat uns belehrt, daß Medizinen von vegetablischen Substanzen zusammengesetzt, dem menschlichen Körper bei weitem dienlicher sind als solche welche von mineralischen Substanzen bestehen.

Das neue deutsche Theater.   New German Theater.

As this remedy has been in use such a long time, it has proven its excellent qualities in cases of sickness, and has saved large doctor's and druggist's bills for a great many. This is, in fact, a remedy which cannot be sufficiently appreciated as a family medicine, which is proven by the testimonials of trustworthy people, of which we have appended a small number.

What are Capuchin-Drops used for?

Capuchin Drops are used principally for such ailments which are caused by colds or impurity of the blood, such as: Hoarseness, Quinsy, Weak Lungs, Inflammation of

Daß diese Tropfen schon so lange im Gebrauch sind ist ein Beweis ihrer Güte und Vortrefflichkeit bei etwaigen Erkrankungen, und haben dieselben schon Vielen große Doktor- und Apotheker-Unkosten erspart. Sie sind in der That ein Hausmittel welches man nicht genug zu würdigen weiß, dafür sprechen die Empfehlungen von glaubenswürdigen Persönlichkeiten, deren wir einige beigefügt haben.

Wofür sind die Kapuziner-Tropfen zu gebrauchen?

Hauptsächlich für solche Krankheiten welche durch Erkältungen oder aus unreinem Geblüte entstehen, wie: Heiserkeit, Halsbräune, Schwäche der Lunge, Entzündung der Leber, Magenlei-

Der Wenzelplatz.   The Wenzelplatz.

the Liver, Stomach Complaints, Indigestion, Cramps, Diarrhœa, Constipation, Inflammation of the Bowels, also for Blood Disorders, such as Impurity of the Blood etc., and the Gout.

The healing properties of these drops are unexcelled when applied for weak eyes, or when the eyes become inflamed, likewise for Catarrhal Sores of the nose, Earache caused by taking cold; good for the hearing, and for hollow or decaying teeth. These drops are also an excellent remedy for healing all Scrofulous Sores, Skin Eruptions of all kinds, Bruises, Cuts, Burns,

For External Use.

den, Unverdaulichkeit, verstaute Winde und Krämpfe, Diarrhöa, sowie Verstopfung, Darmentzündung; ferner für Blutkrankheiten, wie: Blutreinigung, regelmäßige Absonderung desselben und Podagra.

Diese Tropfen sind ganz unschätzbar bei schwachen Augen, Rinnen und

Zum äußerlichen Gebrauch.

Röthe derselben, sowie unflares Sehen. Dann bei Hautverletzungen der Nase und Verstopfung des Nasenkanals; bei Erkältungen des Ohres, woraus Ohrenschmerzen entstehen, Gehörs-Schwäche, und auch bei hohlen oder angefaulten Zähnen. Ferner sind diese Tropfen ein ausgezeichnetes Mittel zur Heilung von Blut-, Brust- und Haut-Geschwüren.

Die Theinkirche.　　The Church of Thein.

Scalds and all open wounds.

A Preventive Against Contagious Diseases.

As a preventive against contagious diseases these drops are to be taken at frequent intervals, but more generally in the morning on an empty stomach. This so thoroughly cleanses the blood, as to render one quite safe from contagion.

By correct use of these drops one will soon find that our assertions are not exaggerated, and that they are of excellent service in ailments and sickness the human body is subject to. Try a bottle and convince yourself.

Quetsch-, Schnitt- u. Brandwunden.

Gegen ansteckende Krankheiten.

Als Schutzmittel gegen ansteckende Krankheiten sind dieselben zu gebrauchen, indem man öfters und besonders früh nüchtern davon einnimmt, indem man dadurch sein Geblüt rein hält und somit vor Ansteckung geschützt wird.

Durch den richtigen Gebrauch dieser Tropfen wird man bald ausfinden, daß unsere Behauptungen nicht übertrieben sind und dieselben in vorkommenden Unpäßlichkeiten und Krankheiten gute Dienste verrichten. Probirt eine Flasche und Ihr werdet Euch davon überzeugen.

Das Rudolfinum.　　The Rudolfinum.

Testimonials

CHICAGO (Lake View), June 18, '89.

Dear Sir:—I believe the Capuchin Drops will save my life.

Respectfully,
ALOIS J. WALSER.

INDIANAPOLIS, Ind., Nov. 25, '89.

Dear Sir:—Your medicine is being used by my son for a chronic stomach complaint with success.

Respectfully,
HERM. HOERST.

GALLIPOLIS, Ohio, Nov. 26, '90.

Dear Sir:—Enclosed please find money order, for which please send Capuchin Drops. After having made some good cures lately, I have been able to introduce same in several families. I have sold the last bottle, and have advance orders for this order. Please send as soon as possible.

With kind regards,
F. JOS. HUND.

....Zeugnisse

Nashville, Tenn., 1. Juni '90.

Geehrter Herr! Senden Sie mir wieder zwei Flaschen Ihrer Prager Kapuziner Tropfen. Ich fand die letzten ausgezeichnet.

Achtungsvoll,
Heinr. Schweiß.

Dunkirk, N. Y., 15. Jan. '92.

Geehrter Herr!—Senden Sie mir gefl. 4 Dutzend Kapuziner Tropfen. Dieselben geben gute Befriedigung, und können nicht geboten werden.

Ihr Freund,
Aug. Kolb.

Ahnapee, Wis., 6. März '95.

Werther Herr Keßler!—Die von Ihnen bezogene Flasche Kapuziner Tropfen haben gute Dienste geleitet. Ich möchte wünschen, daß sie weit und breit bekannt wären für das wohl für ich sie hatte. Ich bestelle hiermit wieder eine Flasche derselben.

Mit Gruß,
Bernhard Döring.

Die Karlsbrücke und die Kleinseite.   The Charles Bridge and the Kleinseite.

HONESTY P. O., Ky., Apr. 20, '92.

Dear Sir:—One of our Sisters has been suffering for years of a chronic stomach complaint. The Capuchin Drops are the first remedy out of many, which have really given her relief.

Respectfully,
BENEDICTINE SISTERS.

KANSAS CITY, Mo., Dec. 4, '91.

MR. FRANK KESSLER.

Dear Sir:—Several friends have strongly recommended to us the Prague Capuchin Drops, after a fair and careful trial, and tell us that it is a most meritorious medicine.
Respectfully,
E. W. JUSTUS.

COVINGTON, Ky., Nov. 21, '93.

Dear Sir:—I have been using the Capuchin Drops for my wife last spring. We have used two bottles, and it has done her more good than the doctor's medicine. The doctor said she had heart beating and a very bad cough, which, he claimed, came from the heart beating. We gave the Capuchin Drops a trial, and they done her more good than all

---

Jeannette, Pa., 26. Mai '94.

Geehrter Herr!—Ihre Anfrage über den Werth der importirten Kapuziner Tropfen habe ich erhalten, auf welche ich wie folgt erwiedere:

Sie kennen meine Abneigung gegen alle Oeffentlichkeit, deßwegen ich auch so lange verweigerte, meinen Namen zu veröffentlichen. Jedoch das Drängen meiner Freunde, sowie auch der Umstand, daß eine gute Sache im Interesse der leidenden Menschheit bekannt gemacht werden sollte, trieb mich schließlich an, die Benutzung meines Namens zu erlauben. Ungeachtet dieser Thatsache, will ich mich kurz fassen, weil meine Aussage genügend Grund für Glauben ist, und ein Versuch, da er nicht kostspielig, kann sich ein Jeder leisten, und sich dann selbst überzeugen.

Die importirten Kapuziner Tropfen gebrauchte ich mit merkwürdig schnellem und gründlichem Erfolg in folgenden Beschwerden:

1. Katarrh, zu verschiedenen Zeiten einen oder mehrere Theile des Körpers angreifend, wie die Augen, Nase, Kehle, Zähne und den Magen.

2. Rheumatismus, welcher die Schultern, Brust und Lunge, die Arme und Beine angegriffen.

Der altstädter Brückenthurm.   The Altstædter Bridge Tower.

other medicines she had taken. If she had not taken the Capuchin Drops she would have gone into consumption. We cannot praise the Capuchin Drops enough. Yours respectfully,

BEN. HOPPENJANS.

CHICAGO, Nov. 12, '94.

Dear Sir:—I have used the Imported Prague Capuchin Drops and find it an excellent remedy for all complaints and distresses arising from the Stomach. I can highly recommend it.

Truly yours
A. W. BREDE.

JEANNETTE, Pa., May 26, '94.

MR. FRANK KESSLER.

Dear Sir:—I have received your letter asking me for my statement relative to the internal value of the Imported Capuchin Drops, to which I reply as follows: You are aware of my antipathy against all publicity, and it is owing to this that I have so long refused my name to appear in public. But the pressure of friends, as well as the circumstance that a good thing should be made known in the interest of suffering mankind, have

---

3. Nervöse Beschwerden, von Mangel an Schlaf, Anstrengung, oder Aufregung herrührend, oder Unverdaulichkeit, welche gewöhnlich catarrhalischen Ursprungs war.

4. Entzündung der Augen, Kehle und Lungen.

Bei einer Gas-Explosion verbrannte ich mein Gesicht, da ich jedoch die Kapuziner Tropfen sofort gebrauchte, so hinterließ dieselbe kein Brandmal. Während ich einst Holz spaltete, flog ein Stück Holz auf mein Auge, durch Anwendung der Tropfen jedoch, wurde der Schmerz bald gelindert und verhindert, daß das Auge schwarz wurde. Da ich in der Handhabung von Messern oder Handbeilen ungeschickt bin, so hatte ich öfters Gelegenheit, bei Verwundungen diese Tropfen zur Stillung des Blutes zu gebrauchen.

Dieses wird genügen, denn wollte ich alle Fälle beschreiben, wovon ich Augenzeuge war, so würden dieselben ein stattliches Buch geben. Aber, der die Glaubwürdigkeit des Gesagten unterrichen möchte, kann von mir Zeugnisse erhalten, welche auch dem Gewissenhaftesten genügend wären.

Hoffend, daß dieses kostbare Heilmittel in jedem Haushalte bekannt wird, zeichne ich

Hochachtungsvoll,

Rev. P. Friedrich, O.S.B.

finally persuaded me to allow the use of my name. But notwithstanding this fact, I will be concise, because my statement is sufficient ground for belief, and a trial, inexpensive as it is, comes within the ability of everyone, and will bring the conviction with itself.

I have used the Imported Capuchin Drops for my own benefit with remarkable quick and thorough success in the following troubles:

1st. Catarrh, affecting at various times one or more parts of the body, as the scalp and forehead, the eyes, the nose, the throat, the teeth, and the stomach.

2d. Rheumatism, affecting the shoulders, the breast and lungs, the arms and legs.

3d. Nervous Troubles, when they resulted from want of sleep, strains, excitement, or from a fatigued or disordered stomach, which generally issues from catarrhal origin.

4th. Inflammation of Eyes, Throat and Lungs.

At one time a gas explosion burned my face, but no mark is left on account of the immediate application of the Drops. At another time, while chopping

---

Beatrice, Neb., 10. März, '94.

Geehrter Herr! — Habe die Kapuziner Tropfen seit mehreren Jahren gebraucht und finde dieselben eine vorzügliche Medizin. (Einer kranken Frau dahier wurde gesagt, sie habe keine 24 Stunden mehr zu leben, weil sie ein Opfer der Lungenentzündung sei. Ich sprach zu ihrem Gatten über diese importirten Tropfen, und sandte ihr eine Flasche. Daraufhin lebte sie nicht nur 24 Stunden, sondern schon 24 Tage. Sie hat jetzt Aussicht zu genesen.

Ergebenit,

Rev. M. M. Merkl.

Indianapolis, Ind., 25. Nov. '89.

Geehrter Herr! — Ihre Medizin wird von meinem Sohn für ein chronisches Magenleiden mit Erfolg gebraucht.

Achtungsvoll,

Herm. Hoerst.

Moorhead, Minn., 28. Jan. '90.

Geehrter Herr! — Ein armer, leidender Mann, welchem ich zwei Fläschen der Kapuziner Tropfen schenkte, kann mir nicht genug danken für die gute Wirkung welche er dadurch in seinem Leiden erhielt.

Achtungsvoll,

Rev. P. Augutin, O.S.B.

Der alte Landtagsſaal.   The old Hall of Diet.

wood, a piece struck my eye, causing very great pain, but this pain yielded quickly to the Drops, and every attempt of the eyes turning black was at once overcome by the Drops. Being awkward in using sharp knives or hatchets, I have had several occasions to stop the bleeding quickly, and cured the injury with nothing but these Drops.

This will satisfy, for were I to describe all and in addition mention the many, many cases that I have witnessed in reference to the internal value of the Capuchin Drops, it would indeed fill a stately volume. Anyone wishing to probe this truth can call on me for all the references that even the most scrupulous may want.

But before concluding I feel bound to express my belief, based upon observation, that a continued use of these Drops for a few weeks will cure the miserable habit of drink, and that it will effect a change in drunkards I have cause to assert.

Hoping then that this precious remedy will become known in every household, I am, Yours most respectfully,
REV. P. FRIEDRICH, O.S.B.

Honeßtn F. D., Ky., 20. April '92.

Geehrter Herr! — Eine unserer Mitschwestern leidet schon seit Jahren an einer langwierigen Magenkrankheit. Die Kapuziner Tropfen sind das erste aus vielen Mitteln, welches ihr wirklich Erleichterung gab.

Hochachtungsvoll,
Benediktiner Schwestern.

Beatrice, Neb., 9. Feb. '95.

Senden Sie mir gefl. ein Dutzend Fläschen Kapuziner Tropfen. Diese Tropfen können nicht genug empfohlen werden. Persönlich gebrauche ich dieselbe für die Kehle und Lunge, und finde dieselben vorzüglicher denn irgend etwas, daß ich je gebrauchte. Für Brandwunden sind sie gerade was man braucht; ich habe sie in einem schlimmen Falle verwendet. Werde die Tropfen unter meinen Leuten einführen.

Achtungsvoll,
Rev. M. M. Merfl.

Davenport, Jowa, 19. Jan. '93.

Herr H. Reißler!

Für beiliegende $5 senden Sie mir Prager Kapuziner Tropfen so bald als möglich. Dieselben leisteten mir ausgezeichnete Dienste vorigen Sommer. Ihr,
Very Rev. A. Niermann.

Der Pulverthurm.   The Powder Tower.

GARRETT, Ind., Nov. 19, '90.

MR. FRANK KESSLER, Chicago.

Send me Capuchin Drops for enclosed draft of $5. The drops have had a wonderful effect here. Respectfully,

REV. A. YOUNG.

TORAH, Minn., Oct. 23, '90.

Dear Sir:—Enclosed $2 for which please send me two bottles Prague Capuchin Drops. The bottle sent to me lately has had good results.

Respectfully,

L. GERTIKEN.

St. Joseph's Church, 6th and High Sts.
BEATRICE, Neb., March 10, '94.

Dear Sir:—Have used the Capuchin Drops for several years, and find it to be a capital medicine. A sick woman here was told that she would not live twenty-four hours, being a victim to consumption. I told her husband about the Capuchin Drops and sent her a bottle. She thereupon did not only live twenty-four hours, but has lived now twenty-four days. She may now recover.

I am, yours truly,

REV. M. M. MERKL, Rector.

Chicago (Late View), 18. Juni '89.

Geehrter Herr!—Ich glaube die Kapuziner Tropfen retten mir das Leben.

Achtungsvoll,

Alois J. Walter.

Covington, Ky., 21. Nov. '93.

Geehrter Herr!—Ich gebrauchte die Kapuziner Tropfen letztes Frühjahr für meine Frau. Wir gebrauchten zwei Flaschen und dieselben thaten ihr mehr gut als die Medizin vom Arzt. Der Arzt sagte, sie hätte Herztropfen, und der schlimme Husten, behauptete er, komme vom Herzklopfen. Wir probirten die Kapuziner Tropfen, und dieselben thaten ihr mehr gut, als alle anderen Medizinen welche sie genommen. Hätte sie die Kapuziner Tropfen nicht gebraucht, so wäre ihre Krankheit in Schwindsucht übergegangen. Wir können die Kapuziner Tropfen nicht genug loben.

Achtungsvoll,

Ben. Hoppenjans.

Chicago, 12. Nov. '94.

Geehrter Herr!—Ich gebrauche die Kapuziner Tropfen. Die Tropfen sind ein ausgezeichnetes Mittel gegen Magenbeschwerden jeder Art, und kann ich dieselben bestens empfehlen.

A. H. Brebe.

Das Altstädter Rathhaus.   The Altstaedter Courthouse.

Beware of Imitations.

Man hüte sich vor Nachahmungen.

The Genuine bear this Label.

Die echten tragen diese Etiquette.

FRANK KESSLER,

SUCCESSOR TO A. LAUSMANN.

IMPORTER AND SOLE AGENT FOR THE UNITED STATES.

378 Orleans Street, CHICAGO.

Pierre-Qui-Vire O.S.B. Salve

✝ ✝ ✝

OF THE BENEDICTINE FATHERS,
SACRED HEART MISSION,
OKLAHOMA.

✝

Price 25 cts. per stick.

THE ingredients and preparation of this Salve, are, and have been for centuries, a secret with the Benedictine monks in France, and its healing properties have been effectually demonstrated. It never fails to cure

Pierre-Qui-Vire O. S. B. Salbe

✝ ✝ ✝

der Benediktiner Väter, von der Herz Jesu Mission, Oklahoma.

✝

Preis per Stange 25 cts.

Die Bestandtheile und Zubereitung dieser Salbe sind, und waren seit Jahrhunderten, ein Geheimniß der Benediktiner Mönche in Frankreich, und haben sich deren heilende Eigenschaften wirksam bewiesen. Diese Salbe verfehlt nie

Cancerous Diseases, Felons, Cuts, Boils, Carbuncles, Tumors, Ulcers, Swellings, Bruises, Abcesses, Tetter, Scald Head, Scrofulous Sores, Fever Sores, and all other diseases of the Skin.

Beware of Imitations of this excellent Salve. None genuine but the one bearing the seal of the monastery.

Testimonials.

St. Francis Hospital,
Lafayette, Ind., April 21, 1887. }
Rev. Father Thomas: —On many occasions we have used the Pierre-Qui-Vire O. S. B. Salve, and it has invariably given satisfaction. With pleasure we recommend it to the public.
Respectfully yours,
Sisters of Mercy.

Krebsgeſchwüre, Wurm am Finger, Schnitte, Schwären, Beulen, Quetſchungen, Flechte, Grindköpfe, Scrophulöſe Wunden, Fieberwunden, ſowie alle Hautkrankheiten zu heilen.

Hütet Euch vor Nachahmungen dieſer vortrefflichen Salbe. Die echte Salbe trägt den Siegel des Kloſters.

Zeugniſſe.

St. Franziſtus Hoſpital,
Lajayette, Ind., 21. Apr., 1887. }
Hochw. Father Thomas:—Bei vielen Gelegenheiten gebrauchten wir Ihre Pierre-Qui-Vire O. S. B. Salbe und war dieſelbe immer zufriedenſtellend. Mit Freuden empfehlen wir dieſelbe dem Publikum.
Achtungsvoll,
Sisters of Mercy.

QUINCY, Ill., July 1, 1887.

VERY REV. FATHER THOMAS, O.S.B.:— For more than four years I have suffered with Tetter on the hand, reaching from the point of the thumb, over the whole inside of the hand. During this time I tried a good many different salves and medicines without finding relief. Two of the best doctors I consulted, pronounced my sore incurable. As a last resource I tried the Pierre-Qui-Vrie O. S. B. Salve, and I thank God, after using it three weeks my hand was entirely cured.

Respectfully yours,
HATTIE TINKLEMANN.

ST PATRICK'S CHURCH,
VERPLANK, N. Y., Sept. 3, 1888.

DEAR FATHER:—I received a severe wound on the leg from a kick from my horse some time ago. I tried everything and could not get relief, until I heard of and used your Pierre-Qui-Vire O. S. B. Salve. Will you please send me $5.00 worth, as I wish to make it known to my people. No one should be without it.

Yours very gratefully,
REV. PATRICK MEC.

Quincy, Ill., 1. Juli, 1887.

Hochw. Father Thomas, O.S.B.: — Seit mehr als vier Jahren litt ich an den Handflechten, welche von der Spitze des Daumens sich über die ganze innere Handfläche erstreckte. Während dieser Zeit gebrauchte ich viele verschiedene Salben und Arzneien ohne Linderung zu spüren. Zwei der besten Aerzte welche ich konsultirte, erklärten dieselbe für unheilbar. Als letztes Rettungsmittel probierte ich die Pierre-Qui-Vire O. S. B. Salbe, und Gott sei Dank, nach dreiwöchentlichem Gebrauch war meine Hand vollständig geheilt.

Achtungsvoll,
Hattie Tinklemann.

St. Patrick's Kirche,
Verplank, N. Y., 3. Sept., 1888.

Ew. Hochwürden:—Vor einiger Zeit erhielt ich einen Fußtritt von meinem Pferde, welches eine schlimme Wunde an meinem Bein verursachte. Ich probierte alles ohne Linderung zu erhalten, bis daß ich von Ihrer Pierre-Qui-Vire O. S. B. Salbe hörte, und dieselbe gebrauchte. Senden Sie mir gefl. $5.00 werth, damit ich dieselbe unter meiner Gemeinde bekannt machen kann. Es sollte Niemand ohne dieselbe sein.

In aller Dankbarkeit,
Rev. Patrick Mec.

We-wo-ka, Seminole Nation, Ind. Terr., Jan. 29, 1887.

Rev. Father Thomas:—There are so many worthless preparations on the market that it does one real good to recommend one that has merit. Such I find the Pierre-Qui-Vire O. S. B. Salve. Having tried it in my practice, I find it superior to all others for healing sores, from fresh wounds to old indolent ulcers. Respectfully yours,

John C. Lowery, M. D.
Nat. Physician for the Seminoles and U. S. Exam. Physician.

Charleston, Ill., Feb. 28, 1888.
Rev. Father:—The Salve you sent has cured a malignant cancer of ten years' duration. Yours most respectfully,
Rev. P. M. Donohue.

✣ ✣ ✣

We-wo-ka, Seminole Nation, Ind. Terr., 29. Jan., 1887.

Hochw. Father Thomas: — Es gibt so viele werthlose Präparate im Markt, daß es mir gut thut, einen Artikel zu empfehlen, welcher es verdient. Ein solcher ist Ihre Pierre-Qui-Vire Salbe. Nachdem ich dieselbe in meiner Praxis gebraucht, finde ich sie vorzüglicher als alle anderen in der Heilung von Wunden, sowohl frische Wunden wie auch alte Geschwüre. Achtungsvoll,

John C. Lowery, M. D.
Nat. Arzt für die Seminolen und Ver. St. Exam. Arzt.

Charleston, Ill., 28. Feb., 1888.
Ew. Hochwürden: — Die mir zugesandte Salbe kurirte ein zehn Jahre altes häßliches Krebsgeschwür. Hochachtungsvoll,
Rev. P. M. Donohue.

✣ ✣ ✣